Praise for *Two Tongues*

'*Two Tongues* is a stunning, masterful debut. Tender and fierce, exacting and generous, these poems herald the arrival of an important new voice. In soulful poems that sing of family, culture, love and community, van Neerven deftly unpicks the brutal colonial stitches that bind this place to history's lies, and lays bare searing, healing Blak truths.' **Maxine Beneba Clarke**

'With defiant truth-telling and with immense heart, Maria van Neerven's poems are generous, uncompromising, humane songs that invite the reader to "surrender to the clay and ash / of this landscape" and to listen deeply. Unpretentiously inventive and utterly real, *Two Tongues* brings family, culture, politics and art into revelatory conversation.' **Andy Jackson**

'Maria van Neerven's *Two Tongues* holds great loss and grief, joy and humour, sorrow and anger. What pulses most powerfully through this collection is great love: of family, of community, of each other. Van Neerven reminds us that the shameful history of this country is always wound into the present, yet her poems resist the cliché of division, choosing instead to interrogate with intelligence and empathy.' **Mary Anne Butler**

'The two tongues in Maria van Neerven's blazing debut spar, laugh and quarrel as they reckon with shame and repair. These are poems that lock under your ribs. Working with fragments, erasures and found texts, these restive, unflinching and necessary poems break and remake form so these tongues can "sing as kin" a Blak poetics witnessing violence and tenacious love.' **Felicity Plunkett**

Maria van Neerven is a Mununjali poet from the Yugambeh nation living in Meanjin. Maria was the winner of the David Unaipon Award in 2023 and was a Next Chapter Fellow at The Wheeler Centre in 2024. *Two Tongues* is her first poetry collection.

TWO TONGUES

Maria van Neerven

UQP

First published 2026 by University of Queensland Press
PO Box 6042, St Lucia, Queensland 4067 Australia

University of Queensland Press (UQP) acknowledges the Traditional Owners and their custodianship of the lands on which UQP operates. We pay our respects to their Ancestors and their descendants, who continue cultural and spiritual connections to Country. We recognise their valuable contributions to Australian and global society.

uqp.com.au
reception@uqp.com.au

Cover design by Jenna Lee
Author photography by Sari Jacobson
Typeset in 11/14 pt Bembo Std by Post Pre-press Group, Brisbane
Printed in Australia by McPherson's Printing Group

University of Queensland Press is supported by the Queensland Government through Arts Queensland.

A catalogue record for this book is available from the National Library of Australia.

ISBN 978 0 7022 7103 8 (pbk)
ISBN 978 0 7022 7265 3 (epdf)

University of Queensland Press uses papers that are natural, renewable and recyclable products made from wood grown in well-managed forests and other controlled sources. The logging and manufacturing processes conform to the environmental regulations of the country of origin.

For my mother and loving family
and ancestors – to give them a voice

‘What does it mean to be held in another tongue.’

Ellen van Neerven

yalany

two tongues

kanna

yalany

yalany

a word
    is

a silent
    note

rooted
    in the mouth

released
    it becomes

an echo
    always

returning
    when i

speak
    out loud

it comes
    back

to my
    birth tongue

yulun

you held
me first
yulun on yulun brown on brown
born to a country
that hides our history passed
down by yugambeh ancestors
only to be brought
out of the cupboard like
fine ~~english~~ wedgwood
for special wht/occasions
our dancers stand
in line to perform like
mission school parades
back then there was
no applause
no standing ovation
skin on skin
brown on brown
i came
from you
you came
from here

kuway

imagine a child   growing up   told your family
are worthless   shame   layers your body as they
pull up   their wht/skin sleeves   to get stuck in

first fleet   carried hatred   to the colony   spread like
all non-native species   entered soil   rivers   bodies
blood   tastes like power   kills everything   that is

beautiful   leaving a legacy   of trauma   if truth came along
spoke kindness   hard to wade   through wht/ghosts in your
head   fighting them   wht/fellas ganging up   on us blak/fellas

in the final throes of despair   voices enter my sleep   kuway
rest with ancestors   on country   inhale the sweet scent
of belonging that   will aways be   listened to right way

jagul

is this our sacred site   we'd ask mum   *no that's far away now*
us blak/fellas live in small community
housing like sardines   she reckons

no good   for big mob like ours
stretch our arms   out the window
to borrow from next door   mum says   *we slept with the stars*

summers were worse   windows wide open
flies heat   we're cookin   mum says
we lived on jagul with our old people   *hunting fishing*
them animal was our mob

them ~~wht/mob~~   took our homeland
all different now   she says
us jahgam askin   *why they do that?*

laughin

wadhun   knew when the   door slammed
racism   entered their home   at school
them kids   makin fun   again of her
daughters blak/fam

askin if they   hunt baked beans   eat witchetty
grubs for   breakfast   those kids   laughin
always laughin   in her room she   lay face
down   on the bed

tears in the pillow   disappearing
wadhun   rises from the kitchen
damper   rosella jam   from aunty
triple favourites   felt   love

what if my mother was born white

i wake to the rooster *what if my mother was born white*
new addition we call him jack *in this colonised land*
i am the only one who hates him *between red dirt and blue sea*
mum's been up before dawn to light the stove *my eyes would no longer be her eyes*
nana yells get up you jahgam for school *my flat nose would no longer match hers*
big porridge pot on the table *brown-skinned nana would no longer be mine*
mum speaks some language *unable to teach me culture sing to me*
nan wasn't allowed to practise her tongue *in the moonlight i dreamt of our shadows*
frightened she'd be taken away she says quietly *as we gut the fish*
we ate nana's damper dripping with syrup *hang them high in dillybags*
her brown-skinned face glows in the fire says c'mon get goin u mob *awaiting dawn*

blak/ghost

our mob have love/hate relationship with them wht/ghosts
us blak/fellas believe in all that unbelievable
hair-raisin s..t our cuz tells the best creepy stuff

mum reckons he shouldn't frighten them littlies wet them
beds like last time us jahgams love hiding
behind pillows screaming runnin amok until

cuz comes lights out get ready he'd say givme big deadly
smiles show them white choppers
he yells so we kin cee-yah

holding our breath in suspense then huge thump hits
auntie's old tin roof us jahgams hidin under
blankets somethin walkin up there big cuz

shirleen calls out nah just them mangoes again us fellas screamin
our lungs out some young ones bawling
minute later laughin again mum shouts

turn it down blak/ghost on the ceiling we yell then finally
waiting is over fav sis-cuz sits in the middle
of the floor torch on his face lowers his voice

gumera

mum yells frustration every morning
from downstairs leaking toilet taps
don't work all these years we're still
not worthy to fix

entered the kitchen for breakfast pungent smell
of last night's tripe clears my nostrils curls
my toes poor people's food they say

for days like statues our drenched towels hung
motionless on the clothesline my mother's three jobs
keep her from what some wht/fellas would

say is important home from school flicked my wet
shoes in the corner to clean up peeled
potatoes looking out the window summer rains

are now a storm made a hot pot of tea for mum
she'll be soaked what do they know about
kinship gumera blak/fella love

anzac

what were you thinking
dad volunteering

for their wwii wht/war their uniforms masking their
shame over your blak/body not seen as an ~~australian~~
citizen yet eligible to die how can we explain ~~wht/~~
~~superiority~~ when they are so ignorant makes

me-so-angry

we're still fighting for our ancestors been here for
thousands of years maybe you were fighting your
own war dad get our country humility back fought
same war without same privileges makes

me-so-angry

unable to walk in anzac parade your bravery love
of country family that's what you were thinking dad
makes me real proud will their ~~wht/gaze~~ be kinder
now than before knowing your blood is red

segregation

crematorium road   forks as you enter
left for wht/veteran   visitors

took right road to   visit my brave biung
was a blak/digger   seen as unworthy invisible

was late afternoon   walked to his grave   covered
in a dark shadow from the   national flag

thought let the world   see   *shame on them*

watched them wht/fellas   carry flowers   heart-shaped
balloons   jesus statues photos some with picnic

baskets to   sit on grass   by their loved one's graves
brought   blu tack   sticky tape   one yellow flower

his fav colour   my two thumbs   pressed hard hoping
it will   hold to the wall   in this heartless place

neutral

our home was a neutral country like   switzerland in the war
only poor blak/family in our street   corner house for all to see

playing with beer bottle dolls   sharing each other's clothes
making mudpie cakes in the dirt   run next door get coins for tv

we were the potato kids   chips mash soup
mum was our miracle cook   conjuring simple to great

outside of our neutral world we became blak and poor

we had no uniforms or shoes   our skin was called dirty
mum was a coloured domestic   unschooled but so intelligent

ironing and washing for wht/people   starched collared shirts
mum stayed up late waiting when   my brother left for night out

would he be beaten or picked up   by coppers jailed like last time
we never spoke of the outside   world but knew the rules

stay clean and tidy   keep your head down
be thankful   don't answer back

balan

was i born angry

bro always angry

says plenty reasons   no entry

for abos just being blak

treated like a caged animal neither

wild nor tame

comes home all bloody

torn fuming from his nostrils

resemble tortured beast

mum would wipe blood from

his face battered

body racism hurts

my family harder to clean anger

comes with sadness

like milk and honey only there's

no sweetness askin

bro which one should

be angrier about depends on

the day maybe whole

family angry birthed to a country

denies sovereignty

of first nations people

don't talk about invasion makes

them wht/fellas real angry

colonisation all over the world

stop banging on

about the past they'd say

mum she's never angry at

them wht/fellas only us

kids not cleaning up says ancestors

spirits lie deep

on country them wht/fellas

can't steal who we are she

knows what to do with

anger makes us jahgam feel real

balan

skin

d o n ' t b e a f r a i d t o l o o k

d e e p e r

dark brown rust darkish dusky

swart soy black oil light almond

smoking hot blak

pitchmen swarthy dark ginger

cinnamon goldstone

never-too-blak blak

tawny snooty coal clove coffee

little-black-dress-blak

sable dim-brunette peanut brown nutmeg

taupe cocoa brown beige tan toffee

blak blood shady shadowy pepper

p e o p l e o f c o l o u r

twilight hazelnut ink-like jet-black

blackish pitch medium spade

ebony blue-black honey-hued raven

onyx jet obsidian

java olive espresso-coloured ochre

garam masala milk chocolate

like golden honey

i t ' s o n l y

y u l u n

three words

don't know the weight of words
only after you tell your brother you feel
the anger ripple through your family

big boy with bloody mouth dripping on his crisp
white uniform watching waiting for the cane to
strike that night warm soda water soothes
his stinging hands and i learn

the meaning of three words
~~guilt~~ for my brother getting in trouble
~~racism~~ for being the wrong colour
~~nugget~~ still don't know why this makes me so sad

new year my brother leaves for high school
i cry on parade feel a familiar push
between my shoulders he was back
hey nugget where's your brother?

kinyingarra

ours   is not a spiritual ritual although
i do   pray on that day for god
to come   save me   almost

every fourteen days   it's pay week
our house just   like us forgets to
breathe as we   wait for my father

to come never   knowing if there
is fury or   calm his rage and
my mother   right to stillness

ten-year-old me understands
the racism of   housing commission
the abuse   from work colleagues
the injustice   for blak/veterans
the refusal of a taxi driver

all have   tasted this blak/curse
of discrimination   anger needs
to go somewhere so   it enters

our house   seeps into the walls
breaks our cups plates furniture
puts holes in doors to

shut out the secrets   destroys
so much   o god can you hear
me under my bed

memories of   the rocky shoreline
with family   my father teaching us
to find   kinyingarra   harvest them

with his   old-fashioned can opener
fill our bellies   remembering   how
i hugged his   long black legs

his wide   smile at mum   as she made
fun   of his front   tooth gap   calling
out loud   show us your   choppers

bangu

words   rush from his mouth tried
to catch them with cupped   hands

askin what's he saying   *gunna buy our land back got bangu now*

he was so high it was just past breakfast   thick clouds
on the ceiling   morning light   filters through ugly   glow

askin   what's he saying   *gunna buy big house for our mob*

i remember him a teenager   hogging only bathroom looking for
the look   like his cousins   brylcreem   slick hair snazzy
sharp clothes   checking all mirrors constantly
what would he see   now?

askin   what's he sayin   *gunna buy what them wht/fellas stole*

postcolonial trauma strapped to his back   dragging

askin   what's he saying   *gunna tell them ancestors to get ready*

cleaned house washed clothes   left spaghetti casserole dish
for them jahgam on the sink he was still   jabbering

askin   what's he saying   *c'mon, you comin?*

as i left my broken   heart on his   sparkling kitchen floor

belong

growing up only wht/fellas had new cars their kids wore shoes
uniforms real tv not coin ones them wht/kids had covered
textbooks pencil sharpeners school bags tuckshop lived
in the true world like on tv us blak/fellas were
struggling didn't belong anywhere i wanted
those things to live without being bullied
stared at called names
our wht/neighbours travelled
on legit holidays bought expensive clothes took drives to the
countryside beach us mob passed billboards that saw shiny
wht/skin teeth blond straight hair snazzy suits big houses
gardens with real flowers them wht/fellas would stand
in their front yard hosing their lawn every night till
dark watching us blak/kids run amok
we were the only family with dead grass
dad's big blak/family would come gambling on the weekend
playing cards for money illegal at the time we'd be raided
police would come lock up my uncles aunties
occasionally my dad we loved our blak/family
they always brought us heaps of gifts
mud crabs curries lollies damper
fruitcake hand-me-down clothes
just like christmas hey
we entertain our well-behaved wht/neighbours hard to
understand why they rather listen/watch our dad
singin out to us jahgam to go around streets
borrow money for groceries till
pay week
mum she shame

malun

seven
days she works three
jobs seven jahgam live
with domestic violence no
way out

heart n soul

tall blak too bloody handsome to be *gay*   aunty says

heart n soul of our big blak/mob   he'd arrive shoutin from the footpath

swinging them hips bum   givin them notorious bear-hugs

us kids' yellin too tight!   kissin everybody lugging watermelon

prawns lollies for us jahgam   letting neighbours know uncle

better not forget them mud crabs again   c'mon you lazy blak/fellas

get out here need a hand   shift them derrières into gear it's party time

us fellas cracking up   aunty reckons always gotta be different

shakin her head   what's that lingo? no stopping our old gammy-leg

aunty hittin the dance floor   holdin back waitin for cuz to cut up

some rugs together they'd   be going for hours the adults

all breathless waitin for bedtime   just when they think last song

old aunt shouts out givme some   *respect* from my girl *aretha*

c'mon aunt cuz says   let's go shake some more leg

us jahgam trailing behind trance-like   coz we loveum

without her

your
door
open
twenty-four seven
enjoyed
your
big
mob
family
them
kids
had
many
troubles
not
those
wht/

ones
blak/
ones
replaced
that
front
doormat
many
times
all
worn
out
mum
says
you'll
miss
me
when
i'm
gone

sis-cuz

x
mas
respite big
blak lunch our
sis-cuz volunteers
as a waiter serving up
big feed roast steam
pudding for them old girls
sounding like thunder wanting
cuz for some yarnin dancin
him dressed to the nines make
up lashes reddest lips g-string
boa feathers them elders
loved it bein real cheeky
slapping his backside
him givin
them jiggle acting
surprised passing
tables showing off
his big smile front
tooth gap our family

trait his father's
and my
dad's too
them
helpers
rolling on
the floor
cracking
up laughin
sis-cuz
growing up
real hard
blak/ gay
the 60s
wht/fellas
no matter
he'd say only
family mob
he's our
deadly
sis-cuz
l o v e
him

warin

was told   by family   'don't listen to news only upset you'
too late   she thinks   his clothes   still hang on the line

relentless   voices pound   inside her head   neighbour's
family calling   for action   she shuts   the windows

two men in uniforms   without name tags   turn up then
walk   away from   her home   back to their lives   families

a split second   she stepped   outside herself
longing to be   somewhere   anywhere

whispered   under her breath   take me too   out of   this pain
his cat   now sleeps in   her bed   does figure eights

around   her legs   while   kettle boils   reach for two   cups
forgot   falls to   her knees   arms point to   the heavens

screaming out loud   not caring who hears   why lord   why
not me   she   lays on the warin floor

searching for   warmth
cat comes   sits
on her back

kawan

shadows disguise   wanna-be
family come   bearing gifts
grins armful of grog to mask
their intentions

whispers behind   closed doors
be careful of that one   fear is
power   pain leaves a trail
stains

in darkness he   abuses
sisters brothers cousins
giddya!   givme kiss

come sit on my lap
call me kawan
call me kawan

kanar

this is not what it is

he loves us

we hide   from the neighbours watching
tv up loud   listening to our house
break in silence

this is not what it is

he loves us

who hears her   but us
who holds her   but us
her body   is not   her body

blame is hers   for the rage
within him   porridge bubbles

in a kitchen with   no chairs

this is not what it is

he loves us

trying to explain kanar

shame

dad can we start
over rewind back to
                          your birth   white sheets
                              over your brown skin
pearl-black eyes so
perfect pure until
                          tarnished   dad can we   fast forward
                             before you were called
nigger before they took
your land identity soul away
                          a black hero in
                                the war   segregated cemetery
is that when the
violence and drinking started
                          were the blows meant
                                for mum or for the
injustice   stripped of
your culture   today who
                                can i blame for
                                the shame of a
                                      father

mih

white casket centred   in a laneway facing paradise
my mum   veiled in flowers love aboriginal flag
me in a daze   longing to jump

up   dance down the aisle   kiss the wooden handle
imagining   her soft face with me again   then racing to escape
for coffee   scones   heaps of cream   her house to
watch b&b   you say to me   there'll be

an ad now us laughing   keeping the fantasy alive
lovely now   lives in   two forever   homes one
behind a rock   with dad   who sits   on a wall
mum   must stretch her neck   keeps   an eye

cemetery on the hill   overlooking her country together
with grandparents'   prime spot   under old oak tree
keeps a mih   on mob's comings / goings
know the footprints

wadhun

when   my mother   died   she left   behind
a woman   who became   a child   an orphan
searching in a   bottomless   world
body   knows
when   things   shift

when   my mother   died   she left   behind
me   running   from   hospital to   escape
reality ringing   her   obsessively   to   answer
hoping   the woman   in that   bed   was not   her

when   my mother   died   she left   behind
me   searching   for the house   that almost   broke us
our   old kitchen   cupboard   stacked with
memories   chipped plates   cups our splintered lives

mum   picked up   the pieces   kept   them
reminder of   her past   or maybe   because
they   were still   useful

when   my mother   died   she left   behind
me   dreaming   wadhun left   a map   on country
to find   her spirit   to bring
home

lemonade

woke to the smell of lemonade scones knew it was my mother
thoughts to remind me of the last thing she baked

for me after all these years still dreaming of her wanting to be
close reimagining us together again when she died

kept one of her dresses in the cupboard engulfed my face to inhale
her scent when black void grips my breath wasn't

her favourite one she said funny how i thought you wore every
summer the flowery one suits you everyone would say

hard to describe the scent of loss even in company but it's
been so long ago people would say grief has

no ears for time nonsense in changing-room mirrors see shadows
silhouettes of you they say i look more like you as i get

older my cheekbones hands skin is your skin i carry you with me
beloved blak mother as you once carried me

two tongues

jalu

fire in my gut
drives
me to rise
above this pandemic of
racism no water can
defuse me

two tongues

lie within my mouth
one blak one wht argue
endlessly

then
laugh and quarrel and
laugh and quarrel

hug each other when cold awaits
the morning sun

then
laugh and quarrel
and laugh and sing and
sing as kin

~~british~~ stole

inherited aboriginal ~~english~~

listen

feel the loss each time i speak

when i tell you

wht/fellas raped our country stole our tongues

first nations blood flows through

stolen land culture children ceremonies language

my veins

you don't look aboriginal

ancestors dna say so

unforgiven

ah queenie … no need for tears it's only the
beginning of what's to come don't cry they may hate
you when they remember how you
forcibly slashed their world left trails of blood & looting
now is the time to grab the wish you
always wanted from your queen mothers stretched-out arms
the gift of compassion regret will win
their favour again … don't look forlorn embrace today
truly i vow your ship will come in everyone
needs another horizon your heart will be full at last
beat so loud the sky will crack open for
all your colonised kingdoms to see you at last don't
forget your isolation tower was a gift
a holiday within your empire some pay heaps of money
for such a prize queenie cheer up your
loyal subjects will return stolen treasures you enslaved
ripped apart displaced from homelands
families culture stories language their stolen children
your tower must be dark lonely here's a gift
to help a large box puzzle called the bigger picture
images of lives you broke into a million
pieces that can never be put back together with a note
unforgiven

qmc

queen mother coloniser
do you sleep at night
while your ships invade
countries of the world
are you jolted from
your sleep awakened
by the terror?

queen mother coloniser
do you sleep at night
while our children stolen
from their beds hear
their mothers sobbing
as you tuck yours safe
in bed?

queen mother coloniser
do you sleep at night
as your young blak
servant pours you jamaican
sherry from her heart
broken cup dreams of coconut
oil her mother combed
through her hair?

queen mother coloniser
do you sleep at night
our old people worry
ancestors' bones are cold lying
in your dark museums far away
from country can you comfort
them like a good mother
should?

queen mother coloniser
do you sleep at night
now you are dead adorned by
your treasures or does the load
of our world you broke
into pieces tighten
around your neck do
your crimes lie heavy
on your chest or do
you just roll over
forget?

shield

~~native~~
~~part – abo~~
~~gin – lamington~~
~~petrol sniffer – nigger~~
~~abo – goggles – jafa – chromer~~
~~half caste – goon – prehistoric – abco~~
~~ninja bludger – ugly – eucalyptus nigger~~
~~koona – simple – vegemite – golliwog – fabo~~
~~blackfella~~
~~tribe – part-aboriginal – primitive – savages – darky – abe~~
~~sooty – quarter-caste – drunks – full-blood – uneducated them~~
~~lazy – leeches – filthy blacks – scum – nugget – jacki-jaki – low class~~

first nations ancestors the oldest continuous civilisation on earth

weapon maker – astronomy reader – artists – desert knowledge
skilful hunter – tool maker – bush tucker food – family kinship
knowledge of country – control burning – control harvesting
ceremonies – dreamtime stories – totems – 250 languages

now we are civilised

cars – planes – netflix – tv – mobile – pc – gym – cafes
technology – moon trips – big w – houses – school
woolworths – designer wear – racism – palaces
queen – king – imperialism – massacres
apartheid – segregation – power
bigotry – taken – stolen land
invasion

exemption
exemption
exemption meant speaking only in ~~english~~
clean courteous *exemption* meant always being
exemption meant to live independently everyday
freedoms and choices *exemption* meant promised including access to
education, health services *exemption* meant
swimming pools and pubs *exemption* meant housing, employment and public
exemption meant entry of venues
away from the welfare *exemption* meant keep children safe
everywhere and far from just *exemption* varied from state to state but it was difficult
their identity and ties to kin *exemption* individuals were required to relinquish language
(1897–1970s) aboriginal *exemption* was a historical policy
exemption
exemption
exemption
exemption
exemption
unjustifiable

imperial delusion

after 'captain james cook' by nathaniel dance, 1776

a dank cabin   small window

looking

out to sea

his body   empowered   in imperial

cloth of night velvet   bound by

black pitch   fine steel threads

fan the crown   of his head   barely

hides   his white stoney face

charts lie

on a tiny table   he sits   in almost darkness

right-hand finger pointing

to the delusion

of the southern ocean

~~queen~~ who split our world into pieces

devil dust   swirls   lifts   mulla mulla
flowers fall   covers church courtyard   in a purple blanket
each morning we sing   ***god save our gracious queen***

wht/fella protector comin
matron say   us kids   should be taught   queen's language
so we sing   ***long live our noble queen***
wet bed   again   punishment
wear   them cloth all day
matron calls me   ***dirty little girl***

wanna   go fishing with   my father
sing with mother grandmother   *just wanna   go home!*

scrub those blak bodies   wht/boss comin
no dirty cloths today spick & span
matron says
we sing   ***god save our queen***

standing on parade hot sun sweat flies   cover her tears
and we sing   ***send her victorious***

kinanbun

been through so much *invasion wars* you & me
funny how you never forgot
us even though we are
mostly out of sight *except for events* bigwig royals
still under your control *despite* being too blak for
tv presenter roles *squeaky clean imagine* hey us mob buy homes
eat mcdonald's *good image* brownie points
for them other counties *lookin on* our blak/art admired
over the world hang in them rich homes
gifted by you to *dignitaries & presidents* proudly presented
authentic ~~english~~ you say
are your kinanbun real wht/master us blak/fellas understand
while you have *eliminated* most of us mob it's
hard for you to remember *our blak/history* as you live
with your smug ignorance under the thumb
of the ~~empire~~ maybe apologise
for being disrespectful
after all what was given to us
unintelligent blak/fellas opposed to what was taken

bargal

cccccccccccccccccccccccccccccccccccicccccccccccccccccc
cccccccccccccccccccccccclivecccccccccccccccccccccccc
cccccccccccccccccccccccccccccccccccccccccccccccccccccc
cccccccccccccccccccccccccccccccccccccccccccccccccccccc
ccccccccconcccccccccccccccccccccccccccccccccccccccccc
cccccccccccccccccccccccccccccccccccccccccccccccccccccc
cccccccccccccccccccccccccccccolonisedccccccccccccccccc
cccccccccccccccccccccccccccccccccccccccccccccccccccccc
cccccccccccccccccccccccccccccccccccccccccccccccccccccc
cccccccccccccccclandccccccccccccccccccccccccccccccccc
cccccccccccccccccccccccccccccccccccccccccccccccccccccc
cccccccccccccccccccccccccccccccccccccccccccccccccccccc
cccccccccccccccccstealingccccccccccccccccccccccccccccccc
cccccccccccccccccccccccccccccccccccccccccccccccccccccc
ccccccccccccccccccccccccccccccccccccccccccccsomeone'scc
cccccccccccccccccccccccccccccccccccccccccccccccccccccc
cccccccccccccccccccccccccccccccccccccccccccccccccccccc
ccccccccchildrencccccccccccccccccccccccccccccccccccccc
cccccccccccccccccccccccccccccccccccccccccccccccccccccc
cccccccccccccccccccccccccccccccccccountrycccccccccccc
cccccccccccccccccccccccccccccccccccccccccccccccccccccc
cccccccccccccccccccccccccccccccccccccccculturecccccc
cccccccccccccccccccccccccccccccccccccccccccccccccccccc
cccccccccccccccccccccccccccccccccccccccccccccccccccccc
cciscccccccccccccccccccccccccccccccccccccccccccccccccc
cccccccccccccccccccccccccccccccccccccccccccccccccccccc
ccccccccccccccccccccccccccccccccccccnevercccccccccccc
cccccccccccccccccccccccccccccccccacccccccccccccccccccc
cccccccccccccccccccccccccccccccccccccccpeacefulccccccc
cccccccccccccccccccccccccccccccccccccccccccccccccccccc
cccccccccccccccccccccccccccccccccccccccccccccccccccccc
cccccccccccccactcccccccccccccccccccccccccccccccccccccc
cccleavescccccccccccccccccccccccccccccccccccccccccccc
cccccccccccccccccccccccccccccccccccccccccccccccccccccc
cccccccccccccccccccccccccccccccccccccgenerationalcccccc
cccccccccccccccccccccccccccccccccccccccccccccccccccccc
cccccccccccccccccctraumacccccccccccccccccccccccccccccc
cccccccccccccccccccccccccccccccccccccccccccccccccccccc
cccccccccccccccccccccccccccccccccccccccccsscccccccccc
cccccccccccccccccccccccccccccccccccccccccccccccccccccc
cccccccccccbargalccccccccccccccccccccccccccccccccccccc

utopia

one of ~~australia~~'s most significant artists kngwarreye
began painting in her late seventies first
female artist to emerge in a movement dominated
by men kame a traditional ceremonial artist
applied intricate designs totems for young
women's rituals using fingers dipped in rich desert
ochres to upper chest breasts arm

anwerlarr dreamtime

yam seed dreamtime was created / long before your birth aunty / founding member
utopia women's batik group / painting sacred designs that / later found your canvases

entangled roots / key food source symbol / resilience nature's life
cycle in the desert / your art spoke love for country / culture / family

i'm writing to you aunty

born on your father's country alhalkere seen as a trailblazer
determined personality

looking at your artwork aunty could see strength as you turned
the angles of your brush only to come back stronger

aunty emily your paintings were so densely packed with layers
of dots that the symbolic underpainting was no longer visible

world scratches their heads asking what her thoughts were
about her art

remembering your brilliant answer

whole lot, that's the whole lot

trophies

waanyi artist judy watson, queensland art gallery

walked slowly to the central   back room wall objects
looked familiar their   shell-like silicon   shapes

illuminated forty   pairs of ears   various sizes nailed on a
stark background   took my breath away   reading horrific

stories of ancestors   tragic blak/history from far north
~~queensland~~ cattle station   where wht/colonisers had

hung collected first nations peoples   body parts on their walls
shocked at the anger of my ignorance   disgust of this

known practice   it's repulsive truth of specimens   called
trophies of war   shipped all over the world our mob   still

waiting for their return to country   my weeping eyes glanced
to right-hand corner   saw little children's ears collated

together as if   finding comfort in their   brutal death
genocide in its   chilling hatred   stared back at me left

feeling   overwhelmed by sadness

jabu

not so way back before dagay came
grt grt grandfather lived on jagan   hunting muni
then all his mob   taken away   to god knows where
them wht/fellas   know where
called protection act   sounds like they care   he says
remembers uncle   who wrote that letter to them
~~englishgovernmentfellas~~
in broken ~~english~~ so they say

pless   mista
don't   know what to   do with my woman
sh   cry cry all day / nighttime
just wanna know when je   gunna bring back our jabu
pless   mista
don't   know what to   do with my woman
sh   cry cry all day / nighttime
pless   mista

grt grt grandfather sad for uncle
no reply

bilin bilin

1800 deebing creek mission

sits in front of his humpy

eyes grieving

his blak skin   is as dark

as their religion

yet he knows blak is no sin

they moulded   him into their whiteness

to convert his   heathen mob

his body loosens

seams begin at the neck

empties all that was scared

crawls away   leaves an empty shell

who gave this despair   made

him slave within their   cause was it

their two-faced tongues

without

mercy that brought   him here

to die

or their ivory god they   speak of

who teaches   right from wrong

in the dreamtime

he wears

no   neckplate

is no longer labelled

blak/king

no   need to ask   permission

like birds free

dreams his way

back home

buhnyi

scared buhnyi trees
hold our ancient memories
of gathering nuts
sharing of stories culture
singing beneath its branches

yarbi

unheard language   replaces the birdsongs
of dulum & wagon   below the rainforest floor
them wht/fellas use names   settlers convicts colony
unknown to us blak/fellas   in this new place
their bodies shout aggression   disdain filthy blaks
by the campfire he hums   thieves under his breath
to the moon who   looks at him in pity
too old to find his   way back was stronger
when younger   missionaries feed them food
but makes him weak   misses roo-tail speakin
his father's language   fishing with mob
in the mountain   stream ancestors watchin over
members sacred   bora-ring his spiritual
ceremony to manhood many   bloods lay below its red soil
watched his father's   painted ochred body totem
feathers upon his head   walking slowly towards him
mother's aunties sang   danced from a distance
met his father's eyes   blade was sharp
felt no pain just   like he told him
night sky was the darkest he   had ever seen hung
like their sin separates   mob from country
he mourns death   what once was

like wht/fellas

got me them exemption papers gunna be like
them wht/fellas
free going home daughter's island wedding
she little
when them ~~protection fellas~~ came member her
screamin
cryin makes me weak thinkin about it bin savin
for present
my girl got me some sharp shoes wannamakeher
proud gunna
go fishin mudcrabbin big mob cook-up traditional way
banana leaves
coverin with sand like aunty taught me she
says you
silly blak/fella gave up your culture family signin
them damn
papers nothin but dog licence lay-down-get-up when they
tell yah
forgot them invaders took everything
them boss now

uninvited

white ship cutting   through black ocean   stood on the
bow as the ship   sailed into cape town harbour
south africa to glimpse the famous mountain   shaped
as a dining table towering above clouds

wht only for dinner   apartheid lives here

blak/south africans lived   forced segregation like
first nations peoples   not that long ago the dock battered
old taxis   lining up with neon   passenger signs

red – blaks only   yellow – whts only

unknowing where to go   followed my wht/friends worried
would i be jailed   is this a time capsule   bad dream being
transported back in time   like my parents oppressed by

chief protector of aborigines

we caught a double-decker bus   to look for a restaurant
city deserted   no blaks after dark   same as my parents
watching for police my anxiety high   can't hide my skin
more signs

blaks – upstairs   whts – downstairs

racism pollutes the air   chokes my throat   fills the atmosphere
with hate and denial   here as in my own country   our sacred
dreaming   lifts darkness   carries truth

no lines

last night went to bed with news headlines
no language could translate
my heart was wrenched
trying to understand civilisation
regardless sun rose
as always even in war

drinking tea watched steam
rise to the ceiling
an ant scrambled up the wall
to a wide crack couldn't cross
lifted my fingernail it hurry
to a hole in the corner to
its family

a simple wish
wanna be with your mob
if only there were no lines
between earth and sky
who can heal wounds scars of the world
blak / people of colour / wht /gender / religion / borders

kitchen window glows sunlight
comforting looked up ant-hole
all is calm
suddenly emotions
empower   my need   to write
to be

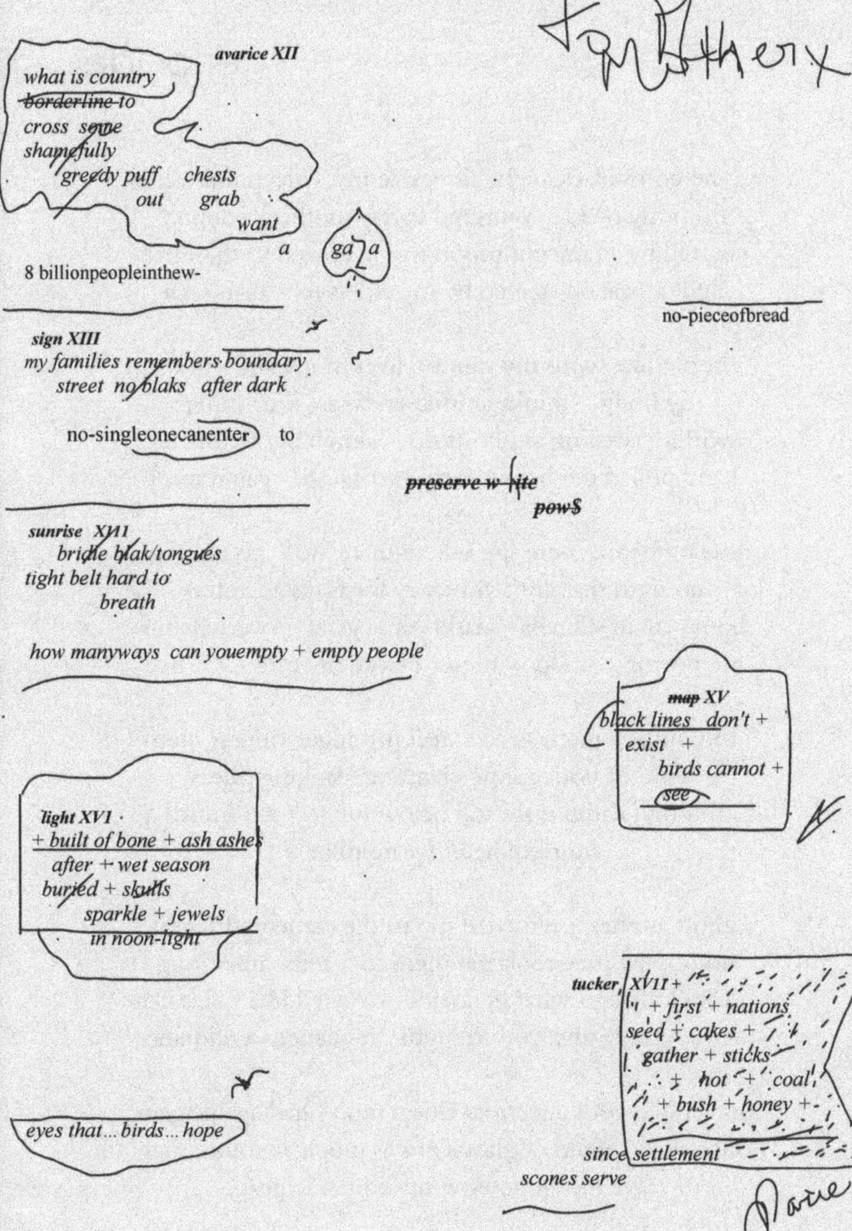

avarice XII
what is country
borderline to
cross some
shamefully
greedy puff chests
out grab
want
a
ga2a
8 billionpeopleinthew-
no-pieceofbread
sign XIII
my families remembers boundary
street no blaks after dark
no-singleonecanenter to
preserve w hite
pow$
sunrise XIII
bridle blak/tongues
tight belt hard to
breath
how manyways can youempty + empty people
map XV
black lines don't +
exist +
birds cannot +
see
light XVI
+ built of bone + ash ashes
after + wet season
buried + skulls
sparkle + jewels
in noon-light
tucker, XVII +
+ first + nations
seed + cakes +
gather + sticks
+ hot + coal
+ bush + honey +
since settlement
scones serve
eyes that... birds... hope

genocide

in the eerie-black night alongside my sleep unleashed
from my bed i ventured to my mother's country
charted by a crescent moon that bowed to the earth
light a beacon steered by my elders to bring me

home like twins my mind lives inside and out of
my body thinking itself endlessly they came
swirling twisting as ghosts do clutch my trembling
hand pulled me below earth surface to pay respect

our mob's massacre site where there are no borders
no signs that say no entry for blaks ancestors
bones lay in stillness darkness as grief overwhelms
me horror stood witness before my eyes i yearned

to embrace them so to feel my anger sadness then
without notice slow chanting singing filters
through damp walls soil below my feet as i smiled
wearestillhere wearestillhere

ghost aunties returned me to the cemented world
askin why they took me there to remember long
not so long ago what genocide looked like felt like
they said to give you strength resilience endurance

power like your ancestors elders mob had again again
once was afraid of ghosts not as much anymore they
leave me alone now since i made peace

kalan

how easy a mind can be   shattered into pieces two days ago
was whole inside now   my worth seems nothing
as their kalan blade   slashes my tongue from   *yes to no*

ancestors once felt their brutality now becomes
mine as they stitch my mouth with wire borrowed
from them other   ~~unwanted~~

was it a flash in the pan idea   *cookie*   when you stepped
from your tall boat   hull full of cannons guns
funded by ~~imperial/whiteness~~ who   saw the bigger picture

first steal their country   ~~massacrepoisonrapemurderapartheid~~
felled like trees   tried to strip us leaf by leaf
hard to get rid of these blak/buggers
squash their spirits   steal their children

so on ~~australia~~ day they   stand proud of this fair just country
hoist the starry flag   sing their ~~wht/anthem~~
them mongrels still trying to kill us

dumped our culture overboard   hoping us blak/fellas would
vanish forever only to be   hauled ashore on our *deadly*
ancestors' shoulders who carried   survival in their dna   *ha*

bumenalah

after m. nourbese philip

data is perfidious albion
evidence first fleet
is the captain
law shooting
is raping
truth massacres

~~*brit/empire*~~ *is*
extreme violence
is removal aboriginal / torres strait children
1910–1970
common is
assimilation
is
policy
economy
is
children / women
is
sexual violence
is
deliberate
is
written
is yugambeh mununjali kombumerri gidhabal
oral
is
blak history
bumenalah

dream delayed

after langston hughes's 'harlem'

why was the dream delayed?

who forgot to feed it
left it to starve belly-up?

what happened to bags of hope on its back
were they too heavy?

burst at the seams left a trail got
lost in the dust?

where were the angels
if all else failed

to fly us to the rainbow with
bucket and spade

then dig for a vision to breathe in
new light?

perhaps we were too late
like a thistle

dried up

with too much blak hate
on its plate

nunany

if they fly in your mouth just swallow locals tell me

nightfall small dinner fires luminate the embankment hungry
camp-town mob sit waiting them dry-river mob
askin in that sign language

whatcha cookin reckon its kanga
their closeness creates longing / sadness for family / my stolen culture

long dark fingers sway like spinifex rising from the riverbed
weaving their yarnin threads dancing to the rhythm of fiery embers

come from coastal mob here i'm a foreigner
we share kinship / blak blood / stories / dreamtime

north side of the river an old traditional man no teeth
barely breathing railed up stomping them skinny legs
shiftin dust won attention from his mob

com gethim givhim nunany
made me weak laughed like crazy

in glorious golden-pink sunset heard them blak/fellas laughin
retelling stories smoke rose to blackness sprinkled in stars
with distinct aroma of roo-tail

kanna

jargal

she escapes
        urban jungle
to mother's jagun /

                        sees white church
                on the hill / calls out to ancestors   *here now*
                                        bin long-long time /

                walks gently
        to grandparent's jargal / sings
                        hoping they can hear her /
sweeps gum leaves from their tombstones /

        scoops
the red soil in her hand /
                plants
        flowers from her garden /

farewells the sky
        with kisses / floods jagun
                        with tears /

                leaves
        her footprints
                where they belong /

dalagan

healing

green leaves scent of

golden lemons its bark

softens waterholes feels like oil

on skin

first jahgam

morning
day before   birth tummy resembles halogen
balloon   am small of frame spitting
image of your blak/nanna could
easily float   to the ceiling just   standing last
night   belly button   popped out looks
like protruding eye   says running
out of space feel this!
        kick

midday
protein levels soaring headaches
worsen whisper
        you'll come early
almost father   feeds me endless apple pie
cravings unaware   you starve inside
        toxemia

evening
unexpected   flow waist down hospital
walls   closing in overwhelming fear
        nurses say *breathe*
like a dutiful child i inhale gassed-
up dreamt you   flying
above slight cut   big pull
        tiny bundle

midnight
oh! *little moon face* gazing
pitch-black eyes shadowing says
please don't leave curled
up like a kitten sleeping beside
me purring smelling milk
my bone-weary eyelids finally
surrender to
    sleep

day after
now-father travels every day to
    nudge
your cheek prompting
to eat afraid staff will forget his
    weak child

weeks later
now a brilliant glow covers
our home hesitant to hold
this amazing joy as hints of
    anxiety guilt still lingers
in the wake of darkness symbolising
light a gift arrives rainbow football
from the dutchies faraway family for
    our shining star

forgive me

if i had said nothing
not returned
your call
left the phone
hanging same
as that cobweb
on the wall settled
to watch deep
pink streaks of
sundown without
a single word bursting
from my mouth watched
thousand small birds
of january
in their soft
soaring cloud
if i had to say something
a tiny tiny thing
well-shaped phrases
smoothed-out edges
as a child's
wooden spoon
    hey
full moon   tonight
your favourite   by the river
us again
belting out tunes
nuruhn

bira

driver's licence finally my jahgam under six
back seats buckled up going to our new
house saying to them

mummy never driven without instructor
before can you pray 'we get there safe'
rear-vision mirrors my son sits

in car seat hands squeezing so tight praying
little white knuckle melts my heart first
time left my young jahgam

two weeks cairns learn nannies's yughambeh
language to make easy for dad school
socks all navy-blue father real

nervous ok i stitched red and green wool no
more mix-ups rang home every day them
jahgam bragging dad

makes best morning teas lunches mcdonald's
lollies no time to chat mum busy
watching tv

wanted to leave silently
via back door did i hug

them tight enough so they know
kiss every wet cheek give

encouraging words like you've
got this repeat list of things they

may forget feed dog etc etc!!!
flew high & fast that day to

escape to the blue mountains to outrun
my guilt freezer was full washing

was done no sore or broken bones
safe for me to bira to me

only son

if they ask where you were born say
you were birthed
by a blak woman who was
smaller
in real life who said
i could be anything a mother's love
despite
her shame is like a heroine
defending
honour some men live by
dreams alone   silly son   you may have
lost
your way on many adventures have
you forgotten we
are
only sure of this
moment

ode to wim

we   have laid   together
forty   years   or more   consistently
right bedside   for you
left   side mine

your descendants
have colonial roots
skin   me blak   bones
blak   history of
genocide / apartheid

our parents   taught
us   well
to live with eyes open   untarnished   by bigotry
we lie   in sync   turn
my back to you   warm

these   cold brown feet
on yours   imagining
our ancestors   what   would they   say

deja vu

all my life there is without   fail an awkward question
shoved in my face sitting   waiting for my kids come
out of school mums'   chitter-chatter about latest
gymwear newest cars subjects i know

nothing of without any indication   where you from
what's your heritage   waiting for an exotic answer
that would   be more   acceptable i'm indigenous
oh, wow thought

maybe greek/south american would've never known
one mum says   then familiar white space   silence
suspends in the sunshade above us hanging
discomfort over me

school bell rang children start   arriving then off to
the playground with their mums & friends   my son
asks can we go mum   they leave   without a word
not understanding he cries

watched tv show beautiful   nine-thousand-year-old
aboriginal rock art west-aust   survived   untouched
by colonisers unlike us   blak/mob question what the
heck should my face look like to them wht/fellas

continually   raped our culture land people   tell me
why lorna j lotus sports bra   is more important
than this country's   blak/history

keep me

after sarah holland-batt

the ~~british~~/language that split your tongue will not keep me
passion for poetry will not keep me
ekphrastic workshops / namatjira paintings will not keep me
the school that hardened your blak/skin & no shoes won't save me
nor the endless need for knowledge
w.b. yeats knows things always fall apart without warning
write a bunch of poems win an award from a clear blue sky
receive online racism that tightens reality around your neck
wondering who has the last word if any is enough
words i chase / run to / follow / fight for / hold dearly escape me now
it is hard to find good words amongst the bad in this
ever-gripping cycle
won't keep me from being discriminated bullied shamed because
they have no identity / follow madness like sheep
won't keep me from reading forbidden literature of poets they
deem ill-suited for their sinful ears they rejoice in the
suffering of others
stop me from speaking our ancient guttural language
voices of poets of all colours / genders that know no boundaries
will always keep me

sink float

anxiety always there no   warning just
a silent swell   like a tidal wave moving
faster than me   when it catches me
i am   stripped of

everything that is me

when did it begin the therapist   asks violence
wakes us from our sleep   echoing mum's cries
huddled under the bed we   wait for the storm
to pass   give it a name   the therapist says

colonisation
segregated
racism
stolen generation
family trauma
postnatal depression

my life becomes smaller   is my past the darkness
that grips so tight   feel its breath on my neck
always stalking me   want to call out my mouth
stings of salt   keep sinking again i am stripped of

everything that is me

not knowing where to   hide or outrun the sadness
closing my eyes, faces of my two young children
appear like a lifejacket   pulling me to the surface
holding me with

everything that is me

blak ~~help~~

here

are some tablets just   takes three months to work suggest
you take up gardening   book a cheap cruise   find a

reliable

person to go with you   pack a straitjacket ensure your
insurance is   paid in advance before you   leave

place

your life on hold for a while send your jahgam to an orphanage
it could   take up to five years or more   tell them to mail

stacks

of pics now   whining to the psychologist they   don't get
much money   make them your friend as your old ones

won't

stick around whatever you   do never   talk to neighbours or
use words like mental health / anxiety-disorder / or

~~being blak~~

you'll have to   move if you do i'm not   responsible sign on
the dotted line can i   have my pen back   see yourself

out

blak enough

after samuel wagan watson's 'love poem'

them **blak/fellas** sayin which side you on cause they feelin **kindamuddled** cause
ain't right colour **not-fair e n o u g h not-wht e n o u g h not-blak e n o u g h**
lookin like i'm squashed in the middle **feelinkindaroughneedsomeearmuffs**
cause i almost had enough of that which-waystuff **notblakenoughblakenoughblakenough**
feelin in a huff / need a creampuff / cause i haaaad / **e n o u g h** of that racist stuff
not goodenough whtenough blakenough fairenough
someone called the **c o p p e r s** put me in jail screamin through **my c h o p p e r s**
with no avail / **queenE** got a whiff made me bail she lookin bit stale **/** reckons justice failed
smackin her lips for some chips n ale / swingin them hips / singin all the way
ye ain't **fair enough-wht enough b l a k-e n o u g h b l a k e n o u g h**
this world has a whole lotta colour—don't matter cause—i'm
blakenough blakenough blakenough blak blakenough blakenough blakenough

being blak 1

my bestie's sixty-fifth
birthday dinner by the sea
family colleagues gathered to
wish her good luck for a retirement
trip to norway gave
her indigenous scarf thrilled
she wore it all night
one wht/co-worker taking
photos came up
to me   hello she says   *i'm a royalist*
before i could say hello
back did i look as if   i wasn't
was it my skin
that gave her permission
to shut my mouth or her colonised blue
blood superior over mine

being blak 2

he lays in the bath
with his jeans on waiting
for them to shrink
to his body wants to look
cool it's saturday night
pay week movie night
out with his wht/mate's pass
his mother's worried
eyes to the bathroom mirror wipes
his cheek from his greasy
hair walking home they get
pulled up hey you
darky come here
outside light has
been on
all night

being blak 3

my son's first day at high school not to be seen
with me i followed from a distance with other
parents weeks later heard rumours of students
circulating comic in the classroom depicting

first nations peoples as drunks / filthy abos / uneducated
/ low class   felt pain for my family and for my son
one afternoon school snacks   lay on our kitchen
table for a gathering of young boys

trying to   become men guzzling coke laughing
out loud i entered   saw them congregating
around the   wretched propaganda on the table
horror is what i felt also calm as they were

still children hello boys did you know i'm indigenous
yes, they   said my son's head   sunk in shame
so this material   is not   welcome in this house
but you are apologies heartfelt remorse was

what i received every time they came back later
reminded my children of their hardworking
family grandparents   they had to be proud of being
part of the oldest continuous civilisation on earth

yilyal

small town

roundabout she lies semiconscious
mumbles
in language no one
understands

pavement burns

her bloodshot eyes staring up
to the sky and unknown
faces full of
contempt

invisible

in dirty clothes matted hair whispering
~~drunken black bite~~# under
their breath
as they

pass

breathing becomes shallow
they step over her refusing
to look for shame
guilt

indifference

echoes

ignored racist comment   watched bold & the beautiful
went for a swim at the beach   came home dry
hope to stop whining   husband shoved sponge cake in his ears
followed marie kondo   first tattoo at seventy
saw bleached coral reaching up like hands   tripped over my tears
put my mouth to the earth   took a bite flossed
found a real wht/friend with a blak/heart   plus two real cats
shouted from highest peak   nothing
went to a wht/collar interview   wore my blak lips
swam ~~english~~ channel   wrapped in first nations flag
baked myself a birthday cake   ate the whole cake
started eating raw   smoked a fish
invited to ~~australia~~ day party   went fishing with mob
stood at the mouth of the river   screamed yes
one wish   racism to stop

threads

this is how   it is //
like moth wings marry the air //
love is a shadow how you lie
and cry after it //
kind of fire that strikes blak
bodies into fever //
rather not speak with history
but history came to me //
we are the same matter
hopes fears and dust //
i walk i breathe on aboriginal country //
call it genocide not colonisation //
out of the huts of history's shame i rise

deadly

enjoying morning coffee   favourite park bench   breathing
in sunlight   sudden abuse pierced my ears   left me

unhinged wondering was my skin the target or my naidoc
t-shirt   before you know racism   you must feel   live it

tourists in awe purchase our blak/artworks gifts for back
home praise our culture then say patronising things like

~~would kill for such beautiful tanned skin probably never burn~~
~~or need sunscreen so lucky then touch your arm~~

return home proudly parading their tanned bodies still holding
hatred for blaks

before you know racism   you must taste injustice   feel its
despair then   swallow to   live another day

discrimination can be   indirect loud unexpected
us blak/fellas know it

bunambil

heat was off the charts   rode my bike to work
sun hung over me saturating my clothes
little boy's mother   shouts

other side of the riverbank in loud
guttural voice to warn

him small ears can't hear big danger coming
too late his cruelty   lives in the entitled
uniform shiny gold buttons soles

of his heavy boots his anger   smells of
righteousness heard bones crunched
child's   screams mother aunty's family running

in shock like me   shouting stop all witnesses
the appalling act   before anyone reached
him big wht/fella who   stood

on little toes walked away laughing turned
his head filthy blak kid   in my way

thousand years

are you filipino spanish turkish?	*no comment*
were you born here?	*on ancestral soil*
is this your home?	*thousands of years*
don't look aboriginal?	*what should i look like*
are you half-caste? one-eighth?	*blak blood*
on your mother's / father's side?	*wake me from this nightmare*
what is your mother's tongue?	*screaming inside*
stolen generation?	*n/c*
do you know your parents?	*look down at my feet – want to run*
your mother born here?	*stop*
can you spell?	*i can spell – no comment*
do you have aboriginality?	*n/c*
why don't you speak your language?	*ask the coloniser's government why*
homeless?	*n/c*
do you want your land back?	*yes please*

fake

after ezra pound

out of the darkness
comes

<u>first line</u> pauses accents   en
jambment

words that keep me awake

lyric dwell
ing   brea k   ing   re   pair

are these words real

hey! this is new

b la k poetry

sounds | snobby | fake
they say it means   *resilience – like bouncing back*

got it
that's cool

will friends be able to sing-along
in poetic suit

fn poets

let truth be told
no more whitewashing //
stories of scars //
sit between 200 pages she
is rarely named //
slinks into a shadowy
world of nothingness //
i screamed into the
spine of the book //
close my eyes wasp's lick my dna //
surrender to the clay and ash
of this landscape // when you really listen
is your listening
deep

kin

week before **yes vote** we   gathered at west end oval for the **yes rally**
sunshine   covered my wet shoulders from the morning rain lifting
hope wondering which god   hailed this sun gift as i   stood
in the allocated s letter with my **yes friends**   taking

proud pics selfies   send to family and friends   news helicopter soared
above   watching us in our **yes t-shirts**   doing the mexican wave
overhead drone here   followed by   attacking magpies
us all laughing i   was in a bubble dreamlike state whole

~~australia~~ was behind us   felt happy brave strong the week that followed
i saw many **yes voters** wearing their t-shirts as voting day loomed
mine was   still in the bag scrunched up under **yes buttons**
stickers information pamphlets we were

supposed to handout too frightened to wear   it without my
yes friends   felt alone scared of   repercussions violence   realising
my minority   in this wht colonised country i   lived in
my elders would be kin of   like i was

dawn

dawn hope rises

sits on my lips like a wish

waiting

to sing its new

sunrise

then

no

by wht/~~australia~~
like a racist slap

Still

the resounding beauty of

our ancient voices

will never be

erased

from our stolen

land it

growls

rumbles at the back of the throat

strengthens

me to sing

again

kanna

who will remember us
but the footprints on country
the ancient songs through valleys
and the stars to guide us home

but the footprints on country
of the lost and stolen children
and the stars to guide them home
end of suffering it will bring

of the lost and stolen children
to see their little faces
end of suffering it will bring
the dance we will dance

to see their little faces
the ancient songs through valleys
the dance we will dance
who will remember us

kali

between cold desert nights
and the threshold of sleep
unsure of when or how poetry found me
my mind was empty
no dazzling thoughts of interest
no scholarly wisdom on my breath
what did i know of words rhyme or
foreign tongue of ~~english~~
not birthed within my blood
there was no singing in my ear
no calling from the hills
only silence
rich scent of myrtle
as i slipped my feet in sacred waters
something touched my soul
swam up into my chest
filled my heart
reached its brim
was inspiration courage
or great-grandfather's eyes on the museum wall
looking back at me
released
hidden spores of poetry
kali
inside me
blak
v
o
i
c
e

glossary

This list of Yugambeh words were sourced from the *Dictionary of Yugambeh* (Pacific Linguistics, 1998) compiled by Margaret Sharpe from various sources.

balan – strong
bangu – money
bargal – pain
bira – fly away
buhnyi – Bunya pine tree
bumenalah – killing, murder
bunambil – boot
gumera – blood
dalagan – myrtle tree
jabu – boy
jagul – native country
jahgam – child, children
jargal – grave
kalan – sharp
kali – this here
kanar – war
kanna – remember
kawan – uncle
kin – shame
kinanbun – native root
kinyingarra – oyster
kuway – come here
malun – big storm
mih – eye
nunany – food
wadhun – mother
warin – cold
yalany – tongue
yarbi – sing
yilyal – sick
yulun – skin

notes

Several poems in this collection have been previously published online or in literary journals including *Aniko Press*, *Best of Australian Poems 2025*, *Meanjin*, *Splinter* and *Westerly Magazine*.

'fn poets' is a cento poem composed of lines from: Ali Cobby Eckermann's poem 'Marrakai' (*Poetry International*, 2011); Grace Lucas-Pennington's poem 'An Arrival' (*Overland*, 2017); Lisa Bellear's poem 'Alive, along Dreamtime' (*Aboriginal Country*, UWA Publishing, 2018); Ellen van Neerven's poem 'Yugambeh and Proud' (*Red Room Poetry*, 2019); Charmaine Papertalk Green's poem 'This is my storytelling!' (*Cordite Poetry Review*, 2021); Natalie Harkin's poetry book *Archival-Poetics* (Vagabond Press, 2019); Jazz Money's poem 'some generosities' (*mark the dawn*, UQP, 2024); and Elfie Shiosaki's poem 'Kingdom' (*Refugia*, Magabala Books, 2024) .

'threads' is a cento poem composed of lines from: Sylvia Plath's poem 'Elm' (*Collected Poems*, HarperCollins Publishers, 1992); Maya Angelou's poem 'Still I Rise' (*The Complete Collected Poems of Maya Angelou*, Random House, 1994); Naomi Shihab Nye's poem 'Burning the Old Year' (*Words Under the Words: Selected Poems*, Far Corner Books, 1995); Mahogany L. Browne's poem 'upon viewing the death of basquiat' (*Poetry*, 2015); Joy Harjo's poem 'Conflict Resolution for Holy Beings' (*Holy Beings*, W.W. Norton & Company, 2015); Candy Royalle's poem 'Threading Battle Lines' (*Red Room Poetry*, 2018); Lisa Bellear's poetry book *Aboriginal Country* (UWA Publishing, 2018); Natalie Diaz's poem 'From the Desire Field' (*Postcolonial Love Poem*, Graywolf Press, 2020); and Ellen van Neerven's poem 'Call a Spade a Spade' (*Throat*, UQP, 2020).

acknowledgements

I am thankful to my wonderful husband, Wim, for his unwavering support of my writing and for being my first reader, critic and patient listener. To my beloved children, Ellen and Ben, whose encouragement, love and support always energised me and my writing.

Gratitude and love to my mother, father, Elders and ancestors for the strength they gave me to listen to my heart and write.

To my excellent mentors for their support, guidance and generosity, I thank you with all my heart: Maxine, Mary Anne, Andy and Felicity. Special thanks to Anna Jacobson for being my first mentor. To my generous women's writing group for listening and encouraging me endlessly, I thank you so much: Sari, Deborah, Anni, Lynn and Sue.

I would like to acknowledge the traditional owners of Meanjin, the Turrbal and Jagera peoples, and also of Kedumba (Katoomba) on the Gundungurra and Dharug nations where many of my poems were written. I am so grateful for Varuna, the National Writers' House, and its staff for all their support and generosity during my stay. You are all dear to me: Veechi, Amy, Mae, Jaala, Anita and all other staff.

Thank you to the Queensland Literary Awards and the David Unaipon Award for making this publication possible, and especially Laura Elvery. Thanks and gratitude to Aviva Tuffield and UQP for their support and hard work to help bring this book to fruition; special thanks to Yasmin Smith for her kindness and patience. Enormous thanks to Jenna Lee for the beautiful cover.

I would like to thank The Next Chapter for their financial support and guidance, especially Xanthea O'Connor who made the whole experience awesome. To the journals who have published my poems, I thank you for your support.

To all the wonderful people and writers I have met on this epic journey of discovering my voice, I thank you.